Preaching Dead In Outer Darkness

Jesse R Bodley

Contents

Identification

Identities were being assigned to a hall of souls,
and mine was being repulsed away from.
So I smiled and said, "let's just be ourselves."
But the others couldn't understand the lack
of trepidation in my acceptance of such stock,
(for being such an attractive and envied spirit.)
I've never wanted to be me and could never
identify with those who could identify with me,
and so I fancied the hull that could be a mask;
and I've worn myself as such for all of my life.

Hay Truck Ride

As plain now as it ever was, or would
have been were we to have seen,
the road goes on falling before us,
as if God saw fit to intervene—each bend,
laughing at our lack of faith;
and all the while, we're in fear
of our own selfish needs.
We softly sang our hymns, passing by
and under this tumultuous wheel,
crashing through the leaves falling
along our path, which once were green,
but now are mulched into topsoil
and covered over by gravel and prayer.

Once Shaken

So damn sacred, it cannot behold the sun rising behind
this presupposed, monumental engraving in cold stone.
The wind shakes the trees once more, and the branches
dance their eternal waving goodbye in the lamp light,
and their shadows only flicker what's on the other side.
Oh, don't whisper—scream out of anger in the night.
Please, God, answer. I have hated you, so.
Not a whisper, the silence holds you close to the dark,
and you wander—and you wonder.
Further out on a limb you climb, far past surmise,
but only once shaken.

All Those Beautiful Dead

Falling asleep into my need to wake up;
waking into a dream—I can't wake up.
Lying very close to the new, as though
right next to you; dying as if old, but young
and cold, though right next to you.
Sinking deep into the abyss that swims
with the dead that can't believe in you.
Alone in this place, with all those who feel
so cold, and old—and so very near to you.
Drowning in a thirst that is so clear, and yet,
crying into a place that used to smother you;
and all the while, wet and fearful of disgrace,
(exposed by another soul to suffer me)
—as I have suffered you.

Funerals

There were days for hours and lots of flowers.
There were so many towers and lots of liars.
There were a lot of prayers, and dreams were mires.
There were ways and roads that led to ours.
We were all so quiet. We were all so white.
We were all together and all quite,
sad and sallow with delight,
(too bad and sad and all so right,)
about a light that ends with night
and sure that peace will come of fright,
when faith would guide us like a light,
although, all blind with perfect sight,
to recompense—for our last rite.

Unbecoming

Dinosaurs, what do you believe in? God is not your savior;
he chose a monkey, and after tossing a rock in your general
—directions are forever, and you cannot see what's coming.
What the hell does forgiveness mean when you can't breathe?
Suppose the moon could reflect on the past.. What then?
Would you have me believe you're not just a black hole; or
can you find it in your fossil records to remember why, the
sky turned to red, to black, to gray, to never-ending; and
why in hell the stars shine when the universe is timeless
in your capsule and memory is dreadful? Beyond alpha and
omega, emasculate the beta—fish; swim for an eternity
in waters overreaching, past and future demanding patience
from them; presently never minding what corners touch them.
Oh, lord of heaven—save this frame or form from torment.
What cost have you decided fate should pay them?
Oh, alcoholism and compassion found time to destroy,
wasted in the furnace of deformed clay and pray—tell, to the
ones you molded from hollow topsoil. Risen from the dead to
bash your evolving brains in. Lap it from the blood of brains
spilled in the depths of troughs; and dogs devour their own
masters, while pigs roast to cinders and wonder why, the air
is filled with stench when death is airborne; and hell
is on the horizon of every vision never asked for.

Sleep Paralysis

You fight the unbecoming, not giving into them. You search
your soul—incoming, no substance in them. These things

have been with us, always—lost, and sinking in; these
dreams are vacant hallways, no quarters within them.

Chosen from birth: selected; cross-examined, then—
overwhelmed (exhausted, all prayers shall go to them.)

If ever you were to choose them, they would leave you.
Only what you seek will ever elude you; only what irks

you could ever be true. These things are only seasons,
and they'll always leave you. Many good reasons—no

good excuse. Are these words pretend? This is the moment
when all thoughts offend. The spirit (always lacking), the

flesh cannot mend. Executioner, god bless you—your
wound is so pure. This is one letter I'll never send. And

you stand the ground alone, the earth, (a spinning head.)
You dig with thoughts unseemly—heaven or hell instead.

Those who've come before you, fell beaten into sin; their
children are monsters; nothing reaches them. The chopping

block is bloody, a basket full of heads, decapitated—
unrated, and their eyes are sunken in—to revelations.

Sheep Amid The Werewolves

I cannot fathom your belief,
(faith in something you can't see.)
I don't know God from atom;
nothing awaits us tomorrow eve.
It never fails as I hear church bells,
my heart shrinks and anger swells
—two-thousand-year-old fairy tales.
Sheep rejoice 'neath cross and nails
—two-thousand-year-old fairy tales.
(Twenty-first century has not a prayer,)
meek little sheep—how they scare.
Behold! 'Neath the full moon, the wolf—Man.

The Pastor Wolf

Awkward in my skin,
at odds with your world.
Why do sheep sin?
A goat's milk has curdled.
Now, I am a wolf—who
is dressed like a sheep;
or am I a sheep—who
is dressed like a wolf?
Cunning and brave—or
senseless and slave,
made to behave
with food you crave?
Led to slaughter
and given no grave.

Werewolf Eyes

Blinded by all your sunlight,
I see better in the night.
Cloudy skies are not enough, I
—eyes see better in the night.
Bathing just outside my shade tree,
unaware what wake, nocturnally.
Under the moon and stars, I hunt thee,
feed on everything denied me.
Eternally unleash inside me,
every shadow cast beside me.

Gag Reel

Never you fear, now—mother dear; never you mind.
There are demons in the world,
(you are right,)
and they are in my mind.
As once it was before the age of light,
in a candlelit room where thespians delight.
Thereupon a stage hung two blind curtains,
dividing in the dark as devils are so certain,
that life is but a play to make of what you may;
and that in the end, the crowd applauds to a line
of bowing frauds;
that we, the audience, are what's real;
and of why we choose to cast our image
through hell's projection reel.

The Sea Gave Up The Dead

These simple people drive a vessel
that is fragile like a glass ship,
made with porcelain sails.
And make claims of a faith which is
more certain than the word, and yet,
upon the slightest deviation off course,
become mutineers of their puppet selves,
demanding tribunals from the depths.

Evolution

Forever left to wonder,
(do we keep some secrets?) Eternal life,
remember? But if madness hath no reason.
What if the lie were true? What will monkey do—up in his high tree,
so high up there—so far down, here in God's country—when he
sees the locust, eating through the world with nothing in the way,
devouring the green, licking every bean—what then?
When will the monkey see—all that the monkey do?

Misfit

Their breath is sweet like honeycomb, and like the birds and the bees they are confused. Their voices are tremulous and often stammering, although, their words—never without benediction.

They are heard wherever they go; they carry a high tone even when low, and always with conviction—and confidence to pursue a hope, a faith, a belief; to spread forth beyond all reason, to fill every darkened cave with light, and make every earthly wrong a right.

(The blessed ones) who have no urge—who feel not the dirge. There are those who from this will purge, whom with their own eyes see through all the lies, those who choose to face demise and never break bread with decadence—and without an aesthetic taste, still from time to time—treat themselves to a drip of honey.

Spiritual Warfare

Oh, my—my heart is broken,
but that's not where it hurts.
My, my—my mind is gone,
and that's just where it starts.
There is a hole,
black as night, black as 'ole,
delaying the whole, the lot
and this damned rot you dare call our soul.
There is a place,
between our placemats and our plates,
to hide all our peas and our beans,
we don't want to eat.
Call it a store; call us a whore.
Call it forgotten childhood lore,
but there is a war—and
its spirited battles are such a bore.

Religious Complaining

Suffice to say—life is not just hard
for everyone, but for anyone.

Who decides who goes where, and
who decides who goes nowhere?

Life is not fair (go figure—and harvest
a pear.) Humanity just needs to grow a pair.

Whoever lived to be so crass? Whoever
decided they were clear to pass?

Salvation is not in mass, but beneath
that very bridge, we overpass.

The Blood Of The Lamb

Saving face,
I hate this fucking place.
Surviving race,
life's a goddamn disgrace.

It's a flood, no.
It's the mud, no.
It's the blood, oh.
A bloody soap sud.

So we wash ourselves,
and we watch ourselves;
we watch ourselves wash away,
and it's our blood and it's their blood.

Interesting how, when among your own,
you feel love,
when evidently—
there is no such thing.

Such Things As Heaven

If we're all still children, then I shouldn't care what beliefs there are in heaven, or if the ones who've made it all the way up there, count their days by seven, or whether they've ever even thought of where this thing comes from—heaven.

And supposing angels require there be air—under their wings to curb depression; or if something you assumed would never dare, belong itself to learning a lesson, for if ever there were a lonesome prayer, another suitor could make an impression.

Because if we're all still children, then our feet are cold and bare, and we're in heaven. And supposing devils inquire as to whether she'll be there, just count down from seven. Because if we're all still children, then we should always beware —such things as heaven.

Interstellar Sadness

That's the sun there. There's another one—not that I believed
mine was the only one. I see a picture, constellations
connecting, blurring my vision

—intriguing someone.
Center on reason; don't lose control. Let us be seasoned,
not worn out and cold.

There's someone's comet burning the sky, like it was
something better than I. Is this in scripture; should we be
afraid? Can't we just wonder and never say?

Certainty as it's seen from this point of view. Seldom
precession, why intervene? This one here, it's that one there;
that one is this one from over there.

Why must they flicker? Can't they understand what just one
is missing? A universe up there, all star systems centered
and falling—but from where?

A Longing For Reincarnation

I don't want to meet the devil,
not unless he knows me at first glance.
I don't want to do good—evil,
not without a girl who wants to dance.
I too could have become people,
but not until I've killed the chance.
I'll be the one to bring upheaval;
we'll see what comes of this romance.

The Devil And The Details

Destroy your grievances
—inside I walk.
Conquer yourself every day.
Life eating, living, dying—decay.
Insufferable silence.
Instances stating flatly,
"employ them,
or let them recall."
Turn over circulation
—ejaculate squall.
Mind overall—a mention.
Immaculate counter
   a wailing wall.

The Voice Of God

I'm so depressed—I can only sleep;
and I'm so ashamed that I can only weep.
I've lost all interest, and I'm no longer me;
I've only regret and want what used to be.

All my thoughts are falling—thirty stories.
All my dreams are blathering allegories.
Inside my mind, there are no goodbyes.
Inside my mind, there are swarming flies.

And each one has an unspeakable vision.
And each one has made a dire decision.
I've become the demon that torments itself.
I've slain the reason—I hate myself.

I should have died before too long;
I should have sung another song.
I want to speak to that voice;
I want to give it another choice.

Life Is Stillborn

Only the starving have something to be thankful for.
The stars are neighbors that want nothing to do with one another.
To microscopic organisms, these are light years between you and I;
and we sing for them who want not for a universe to end,
and those of us distraught enough to find peace
for they have already found it.
They burn the cold and blind the dark
as pulling toward one another's orbit.
It's alright to crush the dead, dry—red leaves
beneath your feet as you walk over graves.
Only try not to kick over their headstones,
which lie near to the place they have prepared for you at their feet.
They won't let me have the whole purpose of existence
(they don't owe me that.)
Much of their silence is instant, and God
is still screaming, he's such an infant.
He was once a man, who much like I,
felt too wrong to be anything other than right.
No sooner does he stand up, he says "fuck life."
No longer does he grow up.
I say alright—the longer I'm a grownup.
I looked up to God and said I hate life,
then felt a bit odd for the rest of my life.

Leaving

A favored god—your god, you're
reaching faith—I'm delving. You are
collapsing in a deep, believing hate.
For all things uncertain—I'm leaving.
We are playing the part—believing.

Insignificance

Must be utterly indifferent, overall
apathetic, to dwell in an oblivion
and not be too absurd.
For when they speak
and/or when they act,
nothing do they press
—never do they seek.
(Just roundabout they go)
in their eternal day-to-day,
in order not to venture far
from the labyrinth womb
—from the well-lit cave.
And though the stars
that shine so bright;
despite the moon
—so full of life,
outside—the world
they've wrapped up tight,
and need never wonder what begot the night.

Outer Darkness

I see too much, and so I close my eyes.
I've heard too much, and so I go blind.
I dreamed of light, and so I lost my mind.
I thought it would never end, and so finally,
it didn't. And now where to, lost out in the dark?
Must fathom reason, have to find a reason
not to make a fire—not to become the flame.

Smoke And Mirrors

I am the worst kind of person, who must be the killer.
I am your least favorite persona, because I'm in your mirror.
Letting go of inhibition: transgressing morality;
decaying with duality; dabbling in divinity.
I am the worst and certainly not the first.
(Sure, you don't thirst—not only to coerce but to be coerced,)
not only by theatrical aesthetics or—ethics;
by laughter, though—as well it is absurd,
to meet face to face with one's own self
and withdraw and exhale from a hit of smoke.
At first, a glance of what was your reflection,
and possibly the climax to all great comedies.

Fall From Grace

I try to fathom heaven
and have to be alone
—afraid to reminisce,
embarassed of a smile.
Must never punch in,
must never redial
—a lost cause in denial.
I'm remiss, and coming
to a realization too familiar,
(encouraging the fire,)
fast approaching—to devour.
Please take it all.
Oh, please make it all
go up in flames and then fall.
We have taken a turn for the worst;
and yet even more foolish,
encompassing a single heading
with bearings lost to an inferno.
Let's say we make a promise;
let's say we take a vow,
to have faith in letting go
—of not only our delusion,
but our denial as well.
And let drift a steady course
—through hell and never force,
surrender but empower,
and watch without anticipation
—and observe the imagination.

Holy Me

It must be hell I deserve, (sure as hell hit a nerve.)
It must be a collision course—I'm on and on.
While the subject is certain, I don't know
a goddamn thing. Is this who I am
or who I want to be? Is there someone inside;
or is he just out there? Is it a possibility,
I am who I want to be? Is this my destiny,
or what I want to be? Do you see in me
a vision not for me? Will you not help me,
the blind who cannot see? Will you not save me
from what I cannot be?

Hallowed Hell

Say, let's too endeavor. Nay, we mustn't fetter.
Hey, it's now or never. Yea, a day is forever.
Forward is backward, and up is clockwise;
take one step further—downward is counter.
It is what it is, 'till it is no more—so take it.
Steal these things from them as well,
and hollow out this hell. Let it go, say farewell,
and hollow out this hell. Home is nowhere;
nothing is there. Anything and of-
course—everything. Anywhere, do we
dare not fare? And so take it with you;
let's burn it all down, and hollow out this hell.

Seemingly

With eyes to see and with ears to hear,
I will become—will not succumb.
I will come to be, (my will before thee)
coming to—becoming, much more
—so much more than all I see.
Without a mind to delve
an endless sea, my spirit suffers greatly,
and wants to be free from all the unhealthy
(moralic acid in thee.) And for all I spare thee,
my message suffers greatly. My vision, though...
Oh, my vision—needs no longer bare thee.
And oh, what has come over me?
The subsequent storm—from a rippled sea.

Flight Or Fight

Is this right? Oh, I don't know what to do, or why I'm here.
Why must a day turn to night, and how high is too high?
I've gone too far, cannot ever go home again.
Contraire, and we start all over.
And again, we gather. Let's stand the timbers—
then, topple them over. Let's marry all the sheep
and then steal their lovers.
Tell them they are innocent, and they will believe it.
Most will submit, although, some will come to posture.
Make them into killers—to fight off the wolves.
Protect only the strong; the weak shall perish.
And keep them moving, it is paramount that they
remain focused away—from this necessary evil.
The good shepherd tends to, and looks over his flock,
in much the same way, the sheepdog only bites
when protecting the herd—but ferociously devours
wolves and sheep alike, when day turns to night
and wrong feels so right.

Tripping On Trees And Dreaming Of Mushrooms

Forever drawing near and never very far—light travels the dark divide alone, as all together see, as through a mirror, lingering down smoky hallways. A wayward soul divorced from God, a detached universe or branching tree.

Flashback to the beginning, a prophecy. The end in a vision of how it came to be. A populace of fleas inbreeding the disease. A pang, a shooting pain through the brain. It's too absurd, or so it has occurred—to be the center of neurological function, and nothing more than thought, existence—too consciously aware of the experiment, a configuration of kinetic calibrations, meaning measured by only purpose and designed by its own parameters.

Unless creation be of dual reality, must stir the flesh into the spirit. What mortar and pestle shall grind the herb and the mushroom together; and what cauldron will brew the potion, the elixir—immortality?

Hamlets

See them there in their world,
churning the milk into butter;
making of the wheat into bread,
the grape into wine—oh, so fine.
See how they all work together,
knowing they are connected;
how they wander in love and kiss,
by day and wake in the night,
fearful of a God that loves them.

Fortuna

A suicide postponed by the unknown, another statistic
proven by wonders, one less wasted casualty of depression
—in youth, a ghost among hosts who tell no truth.

Nightly disturbances and recurring alarms, the whispers
of voices, the sound of a gun. Spatial dimensions warping
with time—malevolent forces and passages mine.

To feel the curling hand of gravity, so strict in its laws
—beyond, conceptual realms and predispositions,
to benevolent plains and heavenly dawns.

Thereby, can perceive of peace, of god—in a moment
of absolute certainty, when atop the wheel; until spun
again, then lose divine consciousness.

Just Like All The Others

God is fattening us up so he can eat us.
He has given man dominion over the earth
and taught us to herd the cattle to slaughter.
He has made us his slaves as we in turn
have made the animals and the trees
and the insects our own.

He is the beekeeper: the dairy farmer;
the shepherd; and the butcher.
And the earth has grown ripe for the
picking—to be plucked from the vine
woven through the arbor.
Then, devoured whole amid the orchard,
the light—of all creation, has shone
too bright: upon the crops; the fields
of grazing cow pasture; the hog farm
and the coop—of chicken caged in squalor.

Bastard, children of Christ, figures of clay cast
in his—our fathers image has built a leaning
tower of glass over oil-stained beaches.
Alas, hail the consumer. God is no architect, rather,
a harvester of souls: another hungry child; another
mouth in this—the garden of eden; and the most
profound and meaningless, paranoid reality.

Tableaux

To hurt—or do we believe in both suffering and relief?
Bereaved, or are we naive—to grieve and not yet leave
the template of our existence at the throne of dissidence?
For peace and all we make believe.
From war, one last fallen leaf.
Redeemed inside the nave,
to peeve—to seethe.

Incomplete Pain

Quickening senses once gave a start, rose the dead from their graves,
pulled the blade from their heart, like an old homeless woman
just a, 'pulling a cart. The lunatic raves, "Jesus Saves!"
A costume cross, so superficial, much like the heart.
Woman, listen good, now—and do come here.
I know of a god, and his name is fear.
Just listen to the tapping of a blind man's cane;
(I'll say it once more, all else is in vain.)
I know, it's too bad—it's insane.
It's too much to bear this incomplete pain.
I know, it's a lot to know the end is near
when you drive alone, too drunk to steer.
Remember us kids looking up at the stars:
one says so very far; one says so very clear,
like embers from a fire, like salt from a tear;
sort of like the first time we kissed and drew each other near,
(much like sharing the last bottle from a case of cold beer.)
I know it hurts; I know about the pain.
I know nothing matters but fire and rain.
So, let's pour from a cloud; let's spill down a drain.
All else is but pain, like crushed cans
in a cart or crutched hands on a cane.
It's just too much to bear this
—incomplete pain.

Original Sin

Paradox has become a paradigm,
for the paragon wastes time,
waiting for their Messiah,
as I am their pariah.
Keeping faith for the peasantry,
braying parables and pleasantry.
The kings reign supreme and entire
over the slaves of an empire.
Morality is the master's key;
he steals their hearts and minds.
False promises of an eternity
have insured success—for his design.
For what an age the gods hath sold
to the withering innocent for a bar of gold,
and such is their place—the masses have given
their souls away to be forgiven.

Serial Killers Rock The Cradle

And they're all so happy now, rewarded for their impudent guidance;
with above all, the utmost dependence from theirs truly—honest
and destitute, the most naive of kind-hearted fools, wavering
with a passionate deceit and the love of a sacrificial lamb.

Chosen from the flock to be led to slaughter; these humans,
they crucify the most noble of souls and burn the most wicked
of hearts. Those whether hot or cold, who offer a new origin
of meaning without doubt in forgotten endings. They breed
their hate (in mediocrity rule.) These sheep—in love with evil,
(they frighten even the wolves,) who scarcely have an acre
to roam. And so hide amongst conformity, secretly bedding
unhappy housewives enslaved by their own dowries, and
lacerated by their own maternal instincts. And the children,
burn down villages in distant lands for honor, then return home
to rule their father's corporation of death and taxes.

Shepherds, sheepdogs, sheep to the bone. Inclined to manipulate
and destroy. Crusaders and holy avengers have spread their seed
throughout the world. Through rape and through war have
enslaved the poor, and through suggestion and lore have made
them want more. Yet, behold. Another "virgin" gives birth
to a son or daughter, half wolf—half sheep, with the face
of an angel, all softened from tears, and the hands
of a madman—all covered with blood.

Damned

Do not tell them—your enemies;
let them see what they have shown.
Only what needs be tempered,
by forge and by fire.

Do not triumph over them but under;
let them believe that they have won.
Should they see you as you are:
not man; not woman; not child;

but demon god in plated armor.
Would that eternal question die
forever, yet live but little—still
resonate with infamy,

in that inferno of infinite night,
as the candle—or the flame
which combusts the moth,
seal the dead in a tomb of wax?

Or else become the contradiction,
or the rule that doubts the exception,
for fear and humility—for redemption.
Cannot even the devil harbor

a secret love for his creator
and all his creation?
Is it not love—this passion,
though lost to the dark?

Have the dead so risen,
as the living have fallen?
Cannot even the damned,
still hope for salvation?

Spree Killers

A shortness of breath spreads a layer of mist
over the saturated soil of a school yard.
The youth in recess play their games,
establishing a much needed pecking order,
developing personalities based on rank
and social stature among the hierarchy,
weeding out the inept and downtrodden
and shoving them to the back of the line,
where their sufferings go unnoticed
and their point of view unrecognized.
There, in the chaos of division and cliche,
where subjugation preserves the roots
of an ill-gotten species of animal,
choking on its own holy sacrament—exists
at a distance, in a remote corner,
where territorial stomping grounds meet
immense forests of unknown supposition,
an arborway through which can only be seen
subtle movement in shadow cast by high canopy
and heard only by those drawn mesmerically toward it.
Those (select few) who are as ghosts,
eloping with forces unseen and bargaining
with something which claims to be eternal,
yet fans out and dies like a wildfire,
and which inscribes an ode with auguries
drawn in the blackened ash
of temporal wastelands,
gnashing its teeth at those who dare
tread its highroad without reservation,

as some children laugh all the while
and welcome themselves into absolution.
Walking away from circular logic,
they delve deep and headlong into isolation,
and find themselves lost to threadbare notions
of things which have not been spoken aloud
or suggested gently in a high wind.
They are the storm; they strike the earth
with lightning bolts and growls of thunder.
Their tears are damaging blocks of hail
that gives you a smile and steals your breath away
with concussions and backdrafts
of exploding momentous ferocity.
Theirs is a lot of extreme terror,
which ought not to be underestimated,
or confused by sentimental security;
their motives are elsewhere—somewhere off yonder
in the burned down ruins of social stigma
and incorrect politics.
Their reason has been all used up;
and they are now the better (whosoever.)

Oh, But Nothing

Not a prayer, but this is getting weird.
If it's all for nothing, goddamn us all.
Give us something, anything, all but
nothing—in a sense. So bloated floating
here, I see nothing but some dead thing,
and that is all. Make it something,
take it back, give it back—innocence,
that is never feared, and one so loving.
Don't let us fall. Make way for a coming;
let'em sing, all but nothing—ignorance.

Puppet Show

Don't tell me what it means. No, I don't want to hear it.
Chemicals control the way I respond to you and pain.
I must infer—why must it matter, if it means nothing?
Molecules commanding fate, the gods are laughing.
They cut my strings, all but one—the one that lifts my head.
The puppeteer is such a child, happy in born ignorance,
drags my feet across the sepulchred earth,
swings my arms about like a horrible merriment.
My eyes roll up to heaven's mandate in a sardonic,
perhaps catatonic questioning—why must it be this way?
A never-ending chaotic cycle, cancer cells make everything.
Where is the location of the soul? Find a surgeon to cut from me
this over-casting infliction. Put my celibate flesh on a plate;
serve it with the placenta with no anesthesia for the brain,
so I can join the feast and be just some dumb thing.
I can't win against this thing; this battle I fight all on my own.
No others seem to grasp the implications. Something hereditary,
now airborne. Some kind of influenza, plaguing everyone.
It tells us it will be okay, then cuts at our throat, bites at our face.
Now I'm being rude—what right do I have to doubt their faith?
I should leave them alone, but I can't continue fighting by myself.
I'm worn out from eating the dead, their animal bones
I toss over my shoulder. Have I consumed their souls
or were they released like smoke from burning daytime fires?
Is this occurrence an act of betrayal? Treason has so many forms.
Should I hang myself as Judas, or will they crucify me
like their Christ, or maybe burn me at the stake?
My heresy knows no boundaries. I spit on the earth as though
in the face of God; my saliva contains so many germs.

I wish to give back this disease but it mutates every time
and becomes pandemic. I'm sure it's the reason for all
world theologies but I can't prove anything—still I know,
like spores come from rotting things, I'm just some rotten thing,
like a manure used as fertilizer, like something pure
condemned and consigned to the fire.

You Worms

Have we now, something else entirely
—withdrawn from reality and reason,
as we all deign, necessary to pretend,
and feign response to trivial things?
Your walking corpses insult me
with every breath they take.

With heaven above, you will drown in a sink
of tepid water like potlucking roaches
fallen from the rim—you worms. I hate you
for all things beautiful that could never exist
in this world, and all things hateful and ugly
that dance for attention and remorse from a god

which never has, and never will be anything more
than a figment of your very poor imaginations.
Your limited faculties preserve with astounding ignorance
—the ivory skeletons from all past atrocities and benefactions.
The dead only sing my song, with silent reverberations
from hollow cadavers—all la la la la la lone.

Imp Gal

If I deserve what I get, then
I've earned what I have taken.
But there's nothing in the world
in the way of value,
and there's nothing but the world,
and it's nothing if not sacred
to those around.
Are we to clothe our naked sin,
or forget what has been taken?
Am I to look upon the world
and take a bow? You
paint a holy—different world,
from blue to black to red,
just look around.
And such gall for you to listen
to the imp you have mistaken
as the beautiful and natural world
that is all around.

Happy Hill

These are very old, phosphorous, and silent
thoughts on their own—their bodies far too cold.
Naked and shivering to shake off their dying,
the mind is wrought with preconceptions,
stirring the void with morose predilections.
Desire feels like razor wire; depression is coal
to fuel the fire—denial is our most basic science.
Digging the earth for the bones of lost souls.
In this, we are alone—subjective concepts,
fighting for the throne of purgatory states of being.
Hallucinogenic alterations taking us higher,
like balloons float—their strings attached
with the very least of earthly concern,
from realms of meaty delight,
to galaxies of heavenly insight.
Out of body, out of mind—
consciousness is winking at us.

Bring Out Your Dead

I have to pick up dead things; I like to pick their bones.
I am here of my own volition; I swept their visions aside.
There can be no mistaking fate—we can deny.
There may be no more presents this late—deified.
I live to pick up dead things; I love to dig their skulls.
I am here, a premonition, screaming all dead inside.
They are all—of another presence, end of an end of late.
Those who never raved, still became—today is one more ride.
I need to dig up said things; I want to fill their holes.
This is fear in recognition of all the dead inside.

Always Defeated

I'll suggest not but I'm warning you,
if it's not an option then it is a fight.
I'm not about to lie down for you.
If I did, I'd die, natural, if not right.
Today, the sabbath—the dead will rise in you.
Not gone to bed, just out of sight.
Pushed too far, no more room for you.
I am the master—just strings pulled tight.
So very long I've been at war with you,
and I'm tired, but still, I'm not out of fight.
Down on the ground swinging up at you,
'cause I can still see even without the light.
I bleed from the tongue, and I'm doing well,
don't have money, but a name, and I say it well.
Some people wonder if I'm adjusted well,
I just say go figure—and go to hell.
I'll tell you what you can think of me,
because if I don't, we may never incubate
fools to build tools for all eternity.
'Cause then how would we ever celebrate
doomsday scenarios—one, two and three?
What if I were to tell you what could never be?
So for once, the two of us can sort of relate,
when you stare down the barrel, and you see me,
I can assure you that I'm no cup of tea.
Peaceable enough, still so full of hate,

and don't think you never had a friend in me.
Fair warning at your funeral—that's my happy place,
'cause I bleed from the tongue, and I'm doing well,
don't have money but a name, and I say it well.
Some people wonder if I'm adjusted well,
I just say go figure and go to hell.
My presence may be unpleasant, but I tell the truth,
and that's more than a lie can ever say for you.
And I don't care for what you say
to try and soothe.
I heard it's not what you say but what you do.
That's just a little something for the old stupid tooth,
in denial of everything—what little you once knew.
But it's alright if your actions are without ruth,
so long as you lay claim 'cross the swooning few.
But you'll find my retaliations perhaps a bit uncouth
when I burn down your cathedral and your last empire too,
'cause I'm not trying to live forever in a fountain of eternal youth.
I will take you with me to the land of always true.
And still, I bleed from the tongue, and I'm doing well,
don't have money, but a name, and I say it well.
Some people wonder if I'm adjusted well,
I just say go figure and go to hell.
Although, the peace of my mind that's about atonement,
has grown out of touch with my recoiling fate.
Peace is a battle and you know it's true—all is unknown,
as such your final resting hole.
Love is a bouquet of flowers for your grave,
they wither and die and overnight, they decay.
Life is a vase of mortals who think they're brave,

they bleed and make others bleed and always go away.
The mind is wrought by cold spells that cannot save
the noonday through the window anyway.
Maniacal ghosts squirm and rash in ancient inns,
no vacancy in the house of the smoking bowl.
No regency in the land of toil, tax and toll.

Primal Sport

Now that you know the game, you can learn the playing field,
and play all by yourself; and if you break the rules,
there's nothing to it really, there's no alternative.
And if your pieces fall, roll the dice even harder.
And if you lose at all, you are out altogether.
So don't go cracking up, your turn will come too soon.
And you can't pass, this time it's offered to you.
And if you can't keep a face, they'll pray a lot for you.
And if you make them laugh, either with or at you.
And if you photograph—well, either way, they'll let you.
And when God becomes a noun, they still won't know you.
So when you go to town, they still won't own you.

Masters Or Gods

Perfect clouds, thunder and rain
—come to take the day away.
You don't take from me; I give to you,
flowers for your grave someday.
I am lightning in the storm; I steal
your calms, even light the desolate way.
I'm the thief, the servant invited.
I am the vampire who sleeps in the day.
We are one—the unrequited,
digesting in the fire of what thrives
in the gray, searching far outside the norm,
reaching back with balmy palms
to write the passage of our way.
You don't make; you ask of me.
Give unto me, the blossoms of depravity.
Darkening darkness, oh—perfect clouds,
sunder and remain, come to take the day away.

Extinction

Lost in space, lost in time,
out passed pluto now, reaching
further—for the hand of god.
He must be waving goodbye.
Eleven hours and counting,
ten—nine—eight—seven,
getting closer to zero.
What specious beliefs
have doomed the species.

Haunted Dreams

Some vague sense coming to an obscure realization.
A spirit asks through delirium,
"do you know what will happen if it makes you feel sorry?"
This cat shedding dies, becomes another ghost visit,
retaining consciousness—no identity, though.
What is it? A question so forthcoming.
How do you feel now that you are all alone?
Why do you worry me, a star—a galaxy?
But in this world, you shone, and maybe we know
who makes up the bed and for sure; or can't we
even empathize—(I could see it in your eyes)
the last breath of some once more;
and now I'm on the cusp of waking up.
So, how is it I'm ready to be gone?
A million stars away—a thousand for a day.
And let us stress no more;
but your silence above your presence
has left such a cold impression.

Startled From Sleep

An old woman once possessed me.
She threw a ball into the woods;
two dogs went in after it
and came out mad.
I rose out of bed in a hurry;
a demon smiled through a mirror.
I thought I heard it say I'm thirsty,
but its jaw hung open and broke.
She can't remember nor can I.
It seemed surprising waking up,
because the very person I called to
in my dream was already there with me.
I do recall a party going on outside,
but what it was for, I don't know—
something about the lost will find me.
I think it's just the heat of summer.
Sometimes I worry but not too much;
I just want to sleep from now on.
No more ghosts or alien visitors,
I thought the dead would stay buried.
I made my way back to bed; I fell into a dream.
This time it was not so weary,
but when I woke up, I was exhausted.

One More Metaphorical Trifle

I come to—woken by the spirits of too high.
The darkness stirs, or nurtures; and I want to die.
Remember the sun; remember the sky,
before I learned goodbye,
before I learned to sigh.
Oh, how could I forget the light:
the earth; the stars; the sight
of the sun, rising to right
the wrongs; the plight?
Before I learned goodnight.
Sunlight beaming—I was only dreaming.
My mind was removed and screaming.
Your son's blood was only streaming,
time internal[Sic] and still dreaming.

All The World Will Know

No surprise and some point of view,
peeking into windows of gabled houses.
Falling into wells and bovine ministries,
many choose ignorance over despair.
Coming to an awareness,
and all—the world should know,
if ever there were a better time for endings,
a flood to nourish these dry and misanthropic seeds;
that given to waste, the land can once again flourish,
if even in darkness for a day, the sun is missed.
So we can finally remember and all—the world could know,
one full hour of their own true nature when all is lost,
and fall down off their high and flying carpets
to land on their big and dumbfounded heads,
where a universe of injustice needs to be imagined
before the blood can spill and all—the world will know.

Manilla Files

Reptilian brain, angel eyes
—mind infirm with global lies.
Unbeliever, sinking tide
—soul corrupted and body died.
No more solemn, stinking pride,
bathe a corpse in shaded light.
Call to heaven while hell beside,
tortured now some haunted nights.
Wasted sermon, the preacher writes
—the word is slurred with golden flies.

The Loaves And Fishes

The loaves and fishes have weekly meetings;
there's a lock on the refrigerator.
I gorged myself on the fill of two,
or maybe three men
I drank until I was drunk but still felt thirsty.
A beautiful woman offers me a smile;
I walk away.

A Poet's Heart

A poet is a heart,
a beating, disgusting
and disease-fearing heart.
And their poems are stomping
grounds for many loathsome
dreams in dark territories.
A poet is bravery, a poet—
His poems are God's words;
he is God's art.

A Little Faith

As much peace flees from me
—a cup of space,
a sip of time.
As such needs be me
—look up to grace,
a trip—divine.
A touch pleas of thee,
lay down some trace
of thee or thine.

The Wrong Man

My soul's not dead,
it's just got holes.
And I'm not lost,
I just don't know
where I am.
Who I am
is not what is—found.
I'm always falling
apart, from the center
of nothing.
Hell, even stars are
exploding,
and what they create
will last a
long time.
I am the wrong man;
I'm living in the wrong time.
I am just a farm hand
and it's tired and withered.
I am the song man,
singing in a low light.

Tempting Fate

Going so fast feels like the verge
—of something, which is slowing down.
 I can speed it up a little, and feel the drag
somewhat less than grinding to a stop.
 I need a plane; I need a jet. I need a spaceship
—a flying saucer. I used to have a dirt bike;
I would risk my life the way I would risk each breath.
I tore up the earth and threw it in God's eyes.
Now, around each bend, I make small adjustments.
I want to crash the wall; I want to throw myself clear
through the next world.

Progress

There is no honor in anything;
nothing is preferable.
The servants are in direct competition;
each master is in league with another.
Slaves are masters of dumb, idiotic slogans.
The flies are sucking vomit;
all lies are built upon it.
There is no truth in believing;
some things are still true.
Might the taste of dust mites have influenced
a dream; or are all things separate?
Have we ever once been faithful;
or have we only sworn to it?
Is our sun really dying?
Is the honey bee dying?

The Knowledge Of Good And Evil

The self is cosmic rape
of the spiritual body.
The swoons are horrendous
and sometimes emasculating,
as an apple taken from the tree.
The flesh is betrayal
of the mind,
copulating disease and entrail,
garnering wisdom from deceit
and harbingering ignorance.

A Moment Of Doubt And Pain

All these things came down from the sky,
angels or demons, and I don't know why.
Nothing matters, and so do I;
nothing is matter—nor am I.
Fell from heaven to light up the sky.
Hard to breathe, and I only sigh.
I want to go home, but first, I must die.

$God And Country$

This is not my home; I've moved too many times from home.
I've come too close to the very farthest reach, and some
parallel dimension I entered without permission, has um—
decided not to recognise me for being so nearly empty.
Too many crowded spaces, too many hiding places,
and not enough of what is considered good for me.

Many generations actualized through one, becoming self
through false pretense, built on tradition and the unerring
belief in the most obtuse and aggrandizing institutions,
which systematically define reality in a compartment
—a cubby hole lotment for the individual who bares
the shelf that stands at the very height of reason. Oh, look
—another simulacrum to replicate objectivity.
So many artistic contemplations, based on nothing.

An observer first believes they are real and then decides
that everything else is real because they—who are real,
can see this thing—which itself is real, when their eyes
themselves do not actually exist. Not a world in itself,
but in which it is—itself believed, by automatons
mass-produced in nuclear families.

Those, who if having raised their right hand and placed
their left hand upon a stack of newspapers, would swear
to the legitimacy of dogmatic law, and later would finger
Jesus as the culprit to a crime. And while praising God
worship only country, and its recurring state which is
supposedly separate from the church but is its former slave.
So, instead of groveling now salutes any flag, so long as
it shares the same basic pattern of evil and injustice.

I Still Remember Those Demons

A man accepts the lack of god's presence
as the rightful evidence of there being no god.
And as a child weeps accordingly, in his aloneness
of being a child, he looks around,
searching the darkness of his bedroom.
I will attempt to explain it—that which I
experienced on a regular basis as a kid.
If one could grasp a paralysis that is tripping.
There is at first an absurd thought, too absurd,
as though not originating from your own mind.
But having been placed there a long time ago,
to occur at intervals, pacing the ridges of sleep.
Alien, this concept—and at that moment,
when you would usually cackle, instead, you focus.
There is a shiver in you that favors no distinction
from hot and cold—a freezing cold fire inside you.
And you feel sick, like someone dying. You feel
nauseous, not from bile but from fear.
Something is coming; you know this.
It's listing toward—flaunting a lack of its own shadow.
Suddenly you remember a past intrusion,
and you can see that this thing knows you,
not by name, you no longer have one of those.
You lie very still, still in the fear—still inside
yourself that comes so near—to what hell is.
That is—your own damned need for certainty.

Fool

Here's this dilemma,
(is it death which requires us
a cure,
or is it that we've demurred;
is it birth which is impure?)
One will pray to God,
and the other will sit
so very still.
Another would starve their self,
and some other will kill.

Join Us Or Die

If only you'll turn, you'll release the chords.
(What a point,) look what I've encountered,
the most intrepid monuments erected til
discounted fortune discontinued benedict.
Connect to destined and tempered tones,
each and separate mounds, swarming one
into desolation. Phoaming, undone, combing
—son, we intentionally condone someone fun.
Put yourself into spin, chew what to continue.
Opinions downward—twin you, past or menu.
Caution totems pin you, or interrupt—segue,
but there's no room, there's no room for thee.

Moralistic Shrug

A lamb, we hate all its stifled breathing, and so looks like we know the feeling—don't we? But it's off the stage or sideways, and it's smeared across our highways, always.

Goddamn, the air is putrid earth of mutant flesh and intellect, a Socratic centerfold—contaminates the bread. So soak our meds in alcohol, or fumigate the stinking air we breathe.

The carpet shows us everything, but tares up from some dry, white wall; and smells of mold and piss and all. Our windows have been left open, but for our curtains.

But if you were me, you would come enticing, you would bring the dying, and taste your sterling menstrual crying. By chance are you alone, or empty? We could dig til someday.

Maybe we could build a—some day. Hiding, enter into some way, we'll say it was the right way, and everyone else will say, Hooray! And then we can all share in a moment of —un-goddamn, bloody likely.

I know Where Evil Comes From

The antichrist was probably a lot like an angel,
or maybe just some sort of good ghost or spirit,
only he must have presumed to be capable of
flying or passing through walls—(not too
unreasonable of an assumption.) But got stuck,
and was cursed by his creator to stub
his toes, and bite his tongue, and spill
ketchup on his shirt, and to be
laughed at by idiots for eternity.
And you just don't understand
why he's so evil, do you?
Well, I guess I don't either,
since sticking up for the devil
might be considered
suspicious by some.

A God I Hate

I hear hell singing up to heaven's mandate, "you are the rock,
I am the flesh, he is the bread, and they are the flock."
God, I hate. God, I hate. God, I hate.

Condemned steeple—what were those people looking up at?
Design is the way: Deployed berserkers, rapists, role models.
Slumped or slouching, someone announcing fate.
What about this thing—or that?
Blow your whistles. Blow your whistles.
What's that in your head; needles sewing holes through thread?
God, I hate. God, I hate. God, I hate—your mind.

You tell me when men lie down inside and resign their heads
to the falling razor; I've done nothing but observe
my own decay.
Enter savior—either favor, we're all so goddamned good.
Hunt or gather—his seed, or slather.
Death does right; the king will kill us to have her.
Oh, you'd rather—you, who gather.
Give your gold away for copper.
Whether clever or clover, cannot commit.
God, I hate. God, I hate, God, I hate—my own.

Sodom and Gomorrah flicker on melting projector screens
like a backdrop of earthly theaters.
We've done little else but delay the sanction of dollars
and doughnuts being dipped in sin.
What could possibly come from billions being clipped
to the pockets of solitary mortals?
The politics of chimps have become corrupted
by the persuasion of the reptilian and the locust.

What species has not discovered this role
of parasites or cancer?
Dominion is the realm
of an ever accommodating evil.
God, I hate. God, I hate. God, I hate—the world.

You leave me scratching paper, whether quill or feather.
Never been deader—let me draw a header.
You called me your angel when I was one disciple.
Let me draw my sword, lord.
Detrimental mental soul-shot, unrelenting continual.
Is this fate sealed with blood wax, written in aether
ink with pen or pencil; are we cross?
What's left over but to decipher visions of an end
that seems to begin forever?
It's getting close now; I'm getting itchy fingers,
clutching pistols, biting crosses, dropping bibles.
God, I hate. God, I hate. God, I hate—fate.

Sewn-in, embalmed with the buzzards 'cause there is none.
What fun in the sun until I'm gone.
Brass steel lead, that's a spiral expanding, hollow gravity
—unnerving swivel.
Point being—holes and heads go together
like smoke and barrels.
How should I tell them your presence freezes fire in place
on a surface of stairs with no level?
Your powers are eternal? I'm either awakened or mistaken.
What could it be if not too late?
What fire could be, but not for me
to burn in the scheme or continue battling?
God, I hate the world.

What Is Happening To Me?

My tongue, it's got frogs, or toads—whichever.
My lung is black, and it's a heart, and it's cool.
I'll let you suck hallucinations from wherever
—you want to taste when you can't feel.

Your visions spread rumors of distasteful answers,
and your dreams are of malfunctioning elevators
and old women who secretly want to choke you.
Their lap dogs got off on the wrong floor and now
they pretend they haven't fallen out with reality,
but if you look closely, you'll see their prescriptions
are outdated and stored on open window sills.
And it's either aggravatingly hot outside
or wet and cold.

Alright then, now onto more suitable topics for discussion.
The opportunity to set things ('a tail spin) correctly,
has flitted by like so many perfections and pretend
connections and prolific derelictions—oh, trust this:
if they're words then they are only words;
if they are thoughts then put them into words;
if they're dreams, then ignore them.

Just don't forget to say the nicest thing possible.
You can say how you really feel once everyone is gone.
Let's not upset one another with things like how we really feel.
Such things aren't really real and what is real is..
It's a good thing our names are put into stone,
while still fresh in our minds so that we don't forget
letters sometimes make sounds.

It's a good thing our tongues are good for more
than just licking our own genitals.
It's a good thing our lungs and hearts are so black,
and we're so cold and burnt out.

What if we took consciousness away from the gods
and gave it to fire wood, or the creatures
that burrow within dilapidated logs?
We should like to swap fluids with the best of them,
and mingle among Troglodytes and Canaanites
and all manner of stag.

We could let Christ turn water into wine and then
nail him to a cross while we all get wasted
and sing his praises long after he's dead.
What if we were to paint the walls
with his blood—a deep, dark red?
Would that make any one of us
any less yellow, or shallow?

Might we, after two thousand years,
finally let him down from the cross
to rejoin his father in heaven, instead
of remaining our sacrificial undead?

I Feel A Reckoning Is Coming

If this is the world I'd be coming back to,
then reincarnation would mean doom.
The only one who can accept you is you;
the only one who can bear to be me is me.
Society confesses to a god it does not believe in,
worships an idol it has conceded.
If death is the inevitable consequence of life,
then life, must of its own inherent nature, be wrong.
I'm going to die, and if I have any say in the matter
—(I doubt it) then, nevertheless, I'm going to stay
dead for quite a while.
No putting the matter on hold
either with a proper burial.
I am to be cremated, and my ashes
are to be spread unceremoniously.
We need to learn how to talk to each other
the way we talk to ourselves.
It's like we're all under some cruel experiment,
and we're all just experimenting
with the lizards and the birds and the insects
that battle for existence in our minds.
Men are the worst decisions ever made
by the fascist gods of some earlier species.
Our saviors convulse away from not only us
but from the very bill of our salvation.
Our kingdoms are orbited by a knowledge
of the living dead and werewolves,
feasting the full expanse of our conscious
and unconscious attention.

One life is none, two lives is one.
Learn the unwritten gospel of sermons
written by the lemur.
Learn the language of doppelgangers and wendigo.
And say goodbye to the lost
and find them reborn through ourselves,
eternally forgiving of one another,
and most importantly, ourselves.
Ask our questions without telling lies,
deal with death without giving our lives.
Listen to the sound we can only hear when
we stop talking and dancing in our toilettes
and graveyards and our pretension of heaven
and accept our nothingness as natural
in the universe without denying everything.
We came here to learn of hell, damn it.
Only then can we dream of a true heaven.
We are the unwitting foot soldiers
of our own primitive form.
No help is coming, and we're either partying
on the roof or praying on the floor.
I forgot all about it, and I don't want
to think about this stuff.
I am being shown heaven
from the highest peak of hell.
My spirit can only know peace after being
set on fire and burning forever.
My eyes scan the heavens beseeching a one true god,
when all around me broils some small understanding.
The world is moving too fast and sees the ground
going by and dumbly thinks that it's change.
I walk away like a suicide note,
only saying that I quit this job.

I ignore my pain long enough
so I can forget what caused it.
I die so that nerve endings
can decay with personality.
I walk away like an apology
(a song sung by all or by none.)

Lacking No Reward

You can't always choose your rewards, not everyone ever can. The servants serve one another—as well they serve the master.

You have a feeling coming on strong; it's overwhelming every second. It's the urgent feeling of having to defecate and vomit.

You looked at some things as being sacred, something that would need to be worked up to. But a few looked at things so casually.

We heard our grandparents say that our generation is mostly desensitized to sex and violence, and the drugs in between.

But the funny thing about the senses is what they sometimes fail to notice, such as reality creeping up beside you.

What makes us think that God is a person? How have we believed in our own arrogance? In what universe would fate preserve us?

A Contradiction

Being sent to hell is cruelty to animals.
We don't even get to know what we're afraid of.
We're born into a world that doesn't know where it comes from
and into a society that only pretends to know where we are going,
when no one even knows what or where we are.
There is no deal bad or good enough to remind me
of how I'm supposed to feel.
A hatred so great as mine and still,
compassion seems to be the only way out.

Too Deep To Mind

Sometimes I turn to wine
for answers to divine
questions that haunt my mind.
Wait your turn, see what you find.
Just let your eyes adjust to the dark
before you look too deep and go blind.

What Of The Dead

I'm doing what I'm supposed to be doing, confusing calms with finalities. I've tripped on every stone and lesson, and survived on one long-winded streak. It's like I saw through a pale of realms and a world was ending, as though the horizon were god's closing eye, with ashes so long they paint the whole world gold, and fan the air so cold they make everything die.

So I'm using a sorcery known as OCD, to escape the universe a person sees when they look at their reflection in the mirror. Oh, the features: all the stars; all the galaxies. I am your profligate—I have to travel you in this body, motor driven by this mind. I see God winking at me in the night sky, then my anxiety leaves me and I feel very tired; and I know that all that happens when we don't die with faith, is that we don't die in peace.

I still have my dreams, which are rather nightmares that I have grown accustomed to. So reluctantly, I have almost denied them. I see my mother there, whereas before I saw my grandfather, or my uncle, or my cousin. She appears suddenly, or suddenly I notice her. And she tries to leave, but I follow her through the house like I did as a kid, asking her questions; those questions have changed quite a bit.

Now I ask if she knows she's dead.
She makes the same expression as she did
in chemotherapy (a shrug and raise of her eyebrows.)
I then ask what it was like to die.
She says, "well, first there was God, and then.."
—and I don't remember the rest of our conversation.
I see my reflection through a mirror, and my pupils
are dilated and then not, and then so. But I still wake up
to the reality of her absence.

This Cosmic Nevermind

There are little lights in the dark; we share the moon on this earth. The sun is ours and we pray to the dirt. The woods keep secrets from travelers; I have stayed there overnight before. A long time ago, when I was you, young and awesome—dwindling notions of sanctity and self, and origins.

Dark and cold expansions in pupiled eyes, witnessing the forest embrace itself in an indistinct but cunning seduction—as with a masturbatory death throw, rattles like a snake and shakes like a dog, but it serves some unseen master. I have suffered a vicious bite, and for whom does my wound dress itself, like a whore in time with tired and beaten genitalia, so caught and tangled in the tatters of a fraught and worldly fringe?

I have died alone, here where you stand. I had at once been mesmerized by sight, so had fallen into blindness from where all light must have come into existence. I don't know that god I once sought; I have forgotten him entirely. I offer you nothing but my conclusion, which resolves itself with zero absolutes. And my naked, shivering betrayal of faith is at once your only guide, but you will come to know me, as I have always known us to be—lost as this, in a darkness deep inside.

Sensitive Soul

Struggle like it matters sometimes,
and look away, conflicted with uncertain
histories, past before a thought occurred.
A thing which is labeled a human soul
and mine has been deeply offended,
or hurt for reasons which are customary,
but nevertheless, cannot be reconciled.
As one of us will turn away, but only
by means of a powerful will, doesn't
look back. Another looks back,
but only to turn away from us.